Th
Real Estate Agent

How to start your career as a residential real estate agent

By Matthew Pichardo

Contents

Introduction

Hello! Thank you for ordering *The Beginner–Real Estate Agent*. Whether you are new agent and not sure where to begin, or you are thinking about becoming a real estate agent and want to get a better idea of what the career will look like, this book will help you along your journey and answer some questions you might have. This book is based on my experiences and knowledge from the San Diego real estate market, along with commentary from experts in the field, their tips, and fun facts. It can also be used as a guide for those newest agents with no connection or background in residential real estate. I hope you enjoy, and most of all, I hope you gain some knowledge that will excel you in your career - Matthew Pichardo

Overview

You might be wondering if it's worth it to get your real estate license--if it's worth your money, your time, and your effort. If you've had any of these concerns, do not worry; this book will give you all of the information that you need. If you have your license and are not established with a brokerage yet, you might be wondering: Why are these people sending me so many letters to join their brokerage? Should I call them? How do I know if that's a good brokerage? What are splits and how do they work? Should I join a team? Along with many other questions. Trust me...I know! Many people start off wondering if this is a career they will like. A lot of people come into the industry because they are good with people, love having their own schedule and being their own boss, and consider it to be a profitable profession. That can be the case, but it takes time to establish yourself. 75% of new real estate agents fail within the first year or two. While this is a fun and exciting job, it is very difficult to begin, and it requires self-discipline, consistency, determination, confidence, and continued education. If you don't have these skills, this may not be the job for you. At this point, we are getting all the negatives out of the way so you can prepare yourself for what's in store and set your expectations accordingly. Like any business, you always want to be the first one in and last one to leave. Expect no checks for 6 months to one year. A sale doesn't happen overnight. Once you find a client, you will go through getting them pre-approved and showing them multiple homes. This usually takes a few months if they are just starting their home search. Remember, it's a lot of money for them and they want to be sure they find the right home. Because the process takes a while, it is recommended to have enough savings for a few months or a second job to keep you afloat. You may also experience anxiety, depression, rude agents and people, lies, and deceit, and you might even consider quitting. Well, you shouldn't. This only makes you a stronger agent. Now that we have covered that, let's move on! So you believe you have what it takes to be a successful real estate agent but you're not sure how to start. Whether you have your license or not, I recommend that you begin interviewing top agents and brokerages. This is very important and will help you get a better understanding from a personal perspective. And for those of you who don't have a license yet, it is recommended that you still take the first two steps. Who knows? Maybe an agent will offer you an internship or part time job as an assistant to gain more experience. That's what happened to me! Let's get started.

Interviewing Agents

You should begin your process by interviewing agents. It's easy to set up a quick meeting with a successful agent in your area and pick their brain, but you have to know who they are and how to find them. It's simple. There are many ways real estate agents can market themselves and their business. Many people search online through Google, Zillow, Trulia, and other similar sites. You will see agents pop up with multiple reviews from clients and their ratings. Write down the names of agents you see that interest you, research more information about them, and if it's someone that seems to fit your ideal vision of yourself, give them a call or send them an email. You can also search by areas you would like to specialize in and ask the agents how they see the market in that area and what the turn over looks like. This refers to the number of homes that come on the market and how fast they sell. Emails usually work best for these types of situations. You'll want to tell them that you came across their page and information and that you think very highly of them. Let them know you are new to real estate and would love to buy them coffee for 10-15 minutes of their time and to pick their brain. It might take a while for them to respond or they may not respond at all, but usually they will be more than happy to sit with you and will even buy you coffee! Yes, free coffee! Also, the meetings may last more than the 15 minutes you asked for. Now you have a meeting set up with an agent and you are ecstatic. But what do you ask them? Be sure to set up questions before hand. Here are some suggestions: How did you get started? Did you grow up here? How did you build your business? How do you get business now? What type of marketing do you do? What do you prefer better, buyers or sellers? What are some bad experiences you've had? Are there any good experiences? What would be something you would change when you first started? What would you recommend I do when I start? And you can add any other questions you might have. Agents are always glad to talk about themselves and tell their story. It's human nature to want to help someone who is really sincere and has the desire to learn.

Hopefully after a few interviews with agents, you see common answers, have a good idea of what to do when you start, and possibly asked them how they chose their brokerage, which we will cover next.

Interviewing Brokerages

So you've got the interviews down with the agents and now it's time to seek out brokerages. But how do you find them and set up interviews? If you've taken your real estate license exam, you may be receiving quite a few letters from different brokerages that want to meet with you and try to get you to work with them. That could be one option. Another option is for you to research brokerages in your area or an area you want to focus on selling. Like before when you set up interviews with agents, you want to call or email the brokerage manager and let them know you are a new agent or interested in getting into real estate and you would love to sit down and learn about the company. I would recommend interviewing at least 5 different brokerages. And yes, I said interview them. It is important for you to have a mind-set that you are seeking a company that will support you and help you grow during your career. Many brokerages offer different types of splits, marketing, in-house teams, and training courses. All these are important for you to understand. Yes, you have to split your commission with the company so you need to make sure the company is worth giving some of your money to. Some questions you may want to ask: What type of marketing do you offer agents? Do you have an in-house title, escrow, and lender? Are there any monthly or yearly fees for the brokerage like E&O insurance? Do you have an in-house transaction coordinator (This is someone who helps you with documents when you're in escrow)? What splits do you offer agents and how do they increase? Are there any weekly sales meetings, and does the broker offer weekly or monthly sales training? How do you think I can benefit from this brokerage? If you are looking to get into the luxury market, you may want to ask: Do you have a luxury division and how is that different? What type of marketing do you offer for multimillion-dollar homes? And so forth. At this point it is up to your discretion to choose the company you believe would best suit you and your needs. Once you've chosen the company, you want to make sure you are there for all the meetings and trainings held, at least for the first few months. You will start to notice a trend of the top producers in your office during the sales meetings. This would be a good opportunity to shadow them or ask them questions. Be wary, some agents are dishonest and unethical and will want you to work with them to take your commission or promise you something. Be sure they are credible and always ask your broker when making decisions like that. It's also good to know as many agents as possible because homes do sell before they hit the market, and an agent in your office could have a listing that suits your buyers.

Affiliates

Both steps above are extremely important for you to do. This will help you get out of your comfort zone and take action on your career and future. That is the most important lesson you can ever learn in real estate: TAKE ACTION! Business is not going to come to you—you have to go get it! Someone is not just going to hand you thousands of dollars, you have to earn it. Now, let's talk about title, escrow, and lenders. Who are they and what do they do? How do they help you and how can you work together? All three of them play an important role in real estate and your business. A title rep makes sure the properties your clients are in escrow with are free of any liens and judgments. Your title rep might also be able to help you with your marketing and farming for door knocking. They can pull up more background detail information on the homes than anyone else, so you want to be sure to have a good relationship with and earn the trust of a title rep that can help you in any way possible. A lender or mortgage broker is the person your clients use to get a loan. There are two possible options. Either your clients will find a lender themselves, or they will ask you for recommendations. It is good to know at least three different lenders and provide them with different options. You do not want to provide a specific lender and them have a bad experience because it will reflect poorly on you. Give them options and let them choose. You are not a lender, you are a real estate agent and you do not have a license to provide them financial information and decisions. That is the lender's job, but it is good for you to always keep track of interest rates and understand how the lending process works. Sit with your lenders and ask them to explain their lending programs and teach you how the rates affect your clients. Escrow is huge! Escrow is when a seller or buyer goes through the process of an offer accepted and the transition of money, inspections, transfer of documents, loan lock, and title process. During escrow many things happen, and they happen fast! Be sure to read over your contract's RPA and any others initiated with the sale. They list all the dates, information, and deadlines you as the agent need to know. Escrow time frame is usually between 30-45 days for a typical finance purchase before it closes and the sale is complete. Some may last longer in other situations, or shorter if it's an all cash deal. It is recommended that you talk to a few affiliates and go through the interview process with them and understand their jobs and duty to help you and your clients. The majority of the time, the seller or seller's agent (sometimes strongest agent) will choose the services escrow and title which is always negotiable in the RPA.

Contracts

You may feel a little intimidated by contracts and figuring out which ones to use. It's your job to know and understand them completely. You should know which ones to use, when to use them, how to use them, and the time frames for your clients. The best way to know these is to print out the RPA (residential purchase agreement), listing agreement, and your agent disclosures. Go through them diligently and highlight time frames you see with one color. With a different color, highlight sentences or paragraphs that don't make sense to you. It can be helpful to sit with your broker and go over these. Besides contracts, you want to know more specific details about the homes. Know the different types of countertops, refrigerators, style of home outside and inside, types of flooring, and if there are any HOA fee's and Mello-Roos fees. You want to know what percent property taxes are. All these will be valuable when you begin to hold open houses so you can answer buyers' questions.

Marketing

Now that we have gone through knowledgeable stages and you have a deeper understanding of what your job entails, it is time to get out there and find you some clients! The key to doing this is to *have a plan*. The first step of being successful in any business is to create systems that work. This is a major task, and unfortunately, most agents don't have the experience and are not sure how or where to start building systems. You need to develop a marketing plan per week and be consistent with it. Since you are a newer agent, an excessive amount of marketing may be out of your budget, but you can leverage all the free sites. Let's go over in detail some options for marketing yourself when you're first starting off.

A crucial part of your marketing is the online presence that you create for yourself. 57% of people searching for homes are using online sites. It's free and easy to create your own profile on sites like Trulia.com, Zillow.com and Realtor.com. It is also a good way to get interaction from other home browsers online and it allows them to see your quality of work. Once you have sales under your belt, you can ask your clients to leave you a review. This helps your credibility and you can use those reviews for your listing presentations and marketing flyers. You should also create yourself a website. There are tons of free website platforms you can leverage and you can even purchase a domain for only a few dollars. Make it catchy, niche to a specific area, or you can use your name. Your brokerage will most likely have their own website so talk to your marketing director and see how you can link them together and what you can do to make yours more appealing for browsers. Finally, create your own blog on your site or another platform. A good use for this is to apply keywords in your writing and on your website. This helps with your ranking online when people search specific words or phrases that match up to what you have written on your page. For example, you write an article of the neighborhood you specialize in and pros/cons of living there, what you love, etc. If a person is looking to buy a home in that neighborhood they will most likely type in homes for sale in X neighborhood. Boom, your article pops up and you look like the go-to expert. It's important to keep your page updated consistently.

Prospecting

Prospecting is the name of the game. Now the exciting part comes. Prospecting is going to be your best friend. There are many ways to prospect like door knocking, cold calls, open houses, events, and mailers. All these points are broad right now and there are some strategies you may find you like or dislike. This is the nitty-gritty for your business. Let's break these down and get you going on taking action.

Door Knocking

This may sound intense but you will gain a lot of value from it. Be sure to have a cell phone with you for precaution or have a friend, partner, co-worker go along with you if you do not feel safe to do it alone. Remember you are door knocking and your goal is to have face-to-face contact with homeowners. Keep in mind that you want to make sure you ask the right questions when you door knock. Practice your scripts weekly with someone and make sure they flow naturally. There are many strategies to door knocking.

- Farming a specific area

Become the expert for that area. Have specific days you go per week or month. Let the neighborhood get to know you and expect you to come. This is a great way to become their go-to agent when they are ready to sell, find a new house, or refer you to someone you can help. I once door knocked and was so nervous when speaking I didn't ask any of the right questions. You can imagine it, it was one of those hi and bye scenarios. The next thing I knew, that same home was on the market a few weeks later. Believe me, I was upset at myself for losing a million-dollar listing, and the listing agent was with the same brokerage! Lesson definitely learned. You don't want to show up empty handed, so get creative with flyers and include market updates for the neighborhood, what the market looks like, anything about their homes they should know, tips for upcoming seasons and how to prepare, how to make your home have a good curb appeal, and so forth. Another option I recommend is to make friends with a local gardener or business in the area such as a restaurant, sports shop, bar, market, etc. that people in the neighborhood go to. You can let them know you go door to door and would like to advertise them on your flyers. Ask if there is any deal they can include encouraging people to go visit. You will basically act as a sales person for them. When you door knock, let the homeowners know there is a coupon on the flyer. This will make them keep the flyer along with your contact information. And on the other hand, you gain a relationship with business owners that could bring you sales.

- ## Knocking before an Open House

Door knocking before an open house in the neighborhood is a great way for neighbors to become more familiar with you. Most of the time you will notice when one home comes on the market, another one will come on within a month or so. It's a trend for homeowners. Let them know who you are. Prepare a flyer with the home details, photos, your contact information, and the open house times. Some homeowners may sound very interested in the home or ask you questions about the value, home upgrades, or other simple questions. This may be an indicator that they are gathering information from you to prepare their home for sale. Ask the right questions and you may have yourself a new listing.

- ## New listings or Coming Soon

Sometimes homeowners don't know about real estate around them. Let them know that XXXX Street just came on the market and you want to know if they want to pick their next neighbor. Ask them if they know anyone who wants to move into the neighborhood. Some may find it funny and appreciate you asking. They may also give you a good lead. Often times they may have a family member looking to move closer to each other. They might also consider moving to a new home in the same neighborhood.

- ## Listings that go pending quickly

This is another great way to find sellers. Usually when a listing goes pending within a week it was priced right and the home or area is desirable for others and had multiple offers. This gets other homeowners in the neighborhood excited because they may gain interest in getting a great price for their home and finding something new. You may want to get insight with the listing agent to see if there were multiple offers and let neighbors know.

- Listings sold recently

If you missed out on any of the options above, you still have an opportunity to let homeowners know the "just sold" in the area, the price it closed at, the average days on market, and how many homes per month are selling in the area. This makes you an expert in their eyes.

Note: If it is not your listing, be sure to ask the listing agent for permission to use their photos and advertise the listing (or take your own) and put disclosures on your flyers. I also recommend that you review with your broker and/or marketing director for their opinion and any disclosures you may need to add for safety.

Cold Calls

If you're great with scripts and being on the phone, this could be perfect for you. Cold calling is not for everyone and denials happen often, but it is a quick way to reach multiple people and save time and gas from driving. Some agents I know only do calls and they are very successful. There are many ways to find phone numbers and get interaction with the people on the other line. You can use cold calling for the same reasons you door knock: New listings, coming soon, just sold, who do you know that's looking, calling expired listings, past clients (maybe not yet), sphere of influence, for sale by owner (FSBO), absentee owners, or a general neighborhood. There are tons of scripts online and seminars you can go to. Your brokerage might even have scripts to give out. Practice and role-play with a friend or agent and have the scripts come natural for you.

- Online Calling Sites

The following online sites are some of the most useful sites for cold calling. They do not all work the same, so most agents sign up for all of them. These sites are used so you can be more efficient and reach more people. This is possible because the system either calls all expired listings, withdrawn listings, for sale by owners, and more. It is able to pull up multiple potential phone numbers and do a constant dial once the line hangs up.

www.colerealtyresource.com

www.landvoice.com

www.mojosells.com

- **White Pages**

I used to use white pages when I first started cold calling because I couldn't afford to pay for the systems. It is somewhat time consuming but also effective. To begin, you can search for an area in your tax records and find the homeowner's name. Once you have the name, log onto whitepages.com and search. From there you want to find the account that seems like it's the right person and try out your chances.

- Title Rep Phone Numbers

Sometimes your title rep might be able to send you some numbers, but don't count on that. Because they deal with more detailed information about the homes and the homeowners, they may have a list stored up. Be sure to double check and not call the "Do not call list" since they are registered.

Open Houses

Open houses take preparation and are the best way to find leads and gain clientele. I cannot stress how important these will be to your career. You want to get this set up early in the week or in advance as soon as you can. You can hold your own listing open or ask an agent to hold one of theirs open. Set this up in advance so the homeowner can prepare the home and so you have enough time to advertise the open house online. Besides the home detail flyer from the MLS, print out a quick summary of all the active listings in the area (detached or attached based on what you are holding open) with no price range min/max. This is valuable to show the buyer other active homes on the market. Obviously a person coming into a condo is looking to purchase a condo and vice versa with detached homes. This is how I found my 3 million all cash buyer who came into my $500k open house. And don't forget to door knock before the open house! Let's go over a few different open house ideas and ways you can prepare:

- ## Open House Signs

You want to have at least 30 minutes before your open house time to set up signs on main streets leading traffic to your open house. Also, don't forget the sign in front of the house! You can also tie balloons on your signs or right in front of the home to get more attraction.

- Food and Drinks

This is not necessary but nice. It shows the buyers coming through that you are prepared and take your time to set up a nice open house and want to accommodate them.

- Advertise Online

Many buyers without agents find open houses online. You always want to make sure the open house is advertised in the multiple listing service and other online sites. If it is not your listing, make sure the listing agent does this. You can advertise on sites like Zillow, Trulia, Craigslist, Open House by Zipcode, and all your social media accounts. If you can, make a video of yourself at the home and describe the details. Post this video to your sites and social media.

- Sign in Sheet

Don't miss out on the buyers who come through the open house. Your goal is to capture their information as a lead if the home is not what they are looking for. A great way to do this is either by pen and paper or if you have an ipad, use Openhomepro.com. It's free, quick, and easy to use.

- Neighbor's Party

This is a great way to get the neighbors to the house and have them extend the invite to their friends and family. Like I mentioned before, usually another homeowner would sell within a short time period so this gives them an opportunity to see the "competition" and get an idea for their home and for you to capture them as a client. They may also have a friend in mind and refer them to you.

- During Your Open House

When you're holding the open house you want to present the home to the buyers that walk in. You want to welcome them and hand them information about the specific home. This should include all the details (number of bedrooms, number of bathrooms, square feet for home and lot, property address, description of the home, and your contact information). If there are multiple people and it gets busy during your open house, greet them at the door, give a brief overview of the home and hand them a property sheet. Let them know where you'll be so if they have any questions they can come ask you. Once they are finished and you see them leaving (if they haven't approached you), you want to catch them at the door, make sure they signed in, ask them what they thought of the house and if it suits them, ask what they are looking for, and ask if they are working with an agent. You don't want to waste your time with buyers who have an agent when you follow up. If there is only one group, you can walk them through the home and show them all the features of the home. It is important to have good body language and tone while doing this. You want to point out all the best features of the home. When showing a room, do not stand in the middle of the room. Your position is important when showcasing the rooms. The best approach is to have them walk in first and you stand to the side of the door. If you're in the middle, the room seems smaller. This is the same case for any room in the house such as the living room and kitchen. It is important to ask them what they think, if the home is what they are looking for, where are they in the purchasing stage, and if they would consider writing an offer. There are buyers who just start looking which is a key phrase for you indicating they may not have an agent yet. At that point you want to create rapport and follow up. Others might be serious and ready buyers but it's possible that they are working with an agent. Some may walk in, not have an agent, and ask you to write the offer for them. SCORE! Anything can happen.

Tip – Most homes on the market will have yard signs in the front on the house with a flyer box. When doing your open house, take the flyers inside so people don't skip coming in and only grab a flyer. Attract them inside and capture them as a lead.

Direct Mailers

Sending out direct mailers can get pricey, but it is a great way to reach multiple people for your new or recently sold listings, finding a home for your buyers, and finding listings. First, I'll let you in on a little secret I used that works for me, but may not work for everyone. I'm originally from Bakersfield, and my friends, family, old colleagues, schoolmates, teachers etc. reside there. Those could be all my cliental! I live in San Diego now, so I had to build my network and business from the ground up. I had my title get the names and addresses of all the people that lived in Bakersfield and also owned property in San Diego and vice versa for those who lived in San Diego and owned in Bakersfield (title can do this by seeing their direct mailing address). So I drafted up a mailer about myself saying who I was, my background of Bakersfield and school I attended, and my new career and my desire to be their San Diego real estate agent. I got tons of positive responses and gained a client here and there. That created rapport between us, and whenever they are ready to buy or sell, they know who they can trust and go to. If you were originally from a different city than where you are working, I would recommend doing this.

- ## Just Listed | Just Sold

Just listed post cards work great for direct mail along with just sold postcards. There are tons of companies that will create postcards for your property that include a description, photos, and your contact information. These just listed or just sold postcards can bring you sellers and/or buyers and are proof to the public that you have the ability to sell in the area.

- ## Buyers Need

If you know your client is looking to buy a specific home by size, pool, lot, area, etc., you have an opportunity to double end if there is nothing you see on the multiple listing service. Have your title rep send you a list of homes that meet your buyer's specific criteria and labels for the homes. Or you can search the tax records and do this yourself. You can type up a Buyer's Need letter and send it directly to the home. (This is a letter that should include information about your buyer, their qualifications, their desire to move into the neighborhood, and what you think is valuable for the buyer.

Don't forget your contact info.) If there is a response, you go to meet the homeowner and see if it works for your client and do a double representation with the seller. If it doesn't, it's a great opportunity to turn that into a listing since they just thought about selling to your buyer. Also, a head's up, when searching for a home and sending mailers, don't forget to check FSBO.

- Listings

This is a great tactic if door knocking is a little intimidating for you and would rather spend the money and time on mailers. You can create and design your flyers to showcase "just sold" homes in the area, market trends, number of active and pending listings, and price points. At this point, you are providing valuable information for the homeowner, and include a little paragraph about yourself with your contact information.

Tip: You will notice the homeowners that usually sell conistantly live in a home for 2-6 years then sell. If a homeowner has owned their home for 7+ years, most likely they are there to stay.

Floor Time

Your office might offer floor time. Floor time refers to being the agent who takes incoming phone calls from your company's ads, signs and Web marketing. You may also have people who stop by in person to inquire about buying, selling, or renting a home who are called "walk-ins." If the office is in a good location with lots of traffic, sitting on floor is highly recommended. People often come in asking questions about homes, and it's a good opportunity for you to help them out. Be sure this is lucrative for you and you are able to qualify the lead and convert them into an appointment. One positive aspect of floor time is that you get the opportunity to work on tasks you will be doing in the office already while having a chance to pick up on any incoming calls or people during your shift. The lead will talk to you about homes so you need to make sure you gather the best information from them. We've talked about qualifying the lead before which consists of where they are in their search, their loan process, what type of home they are looking for in detail, and their price range. If it is a seller on the phone or who walked in, qualify them by getting their address, what their plans are for moving, where they are moving, their time frame for when they would like to sell, and so forth. Set a date with them to view the home and give them a presentation of their home value. This for you is a listing presentation. You are in the process of converting a lead. Always set expectations and your next steps to proceed.

You can choose to do any of the above forms of prospecting. There is no telling which will work best for you until you try. A good way to narrow down what works for you is to see how many leads you are generating for the number of hours spent. If other prospecting activities are generating more leads, then focus on your more dollar-productive activities.

Leveraging Your Schedule

It takes a lot to do all this work, especially when dealing with multiple clients while keeping your current lead generating plan on track. Creating a schedule will be your lifesaver. Again, the systems you have in place need to be consistent and scheduled. This is essential if you have a second job holding you up financially. Once you gain a book of clientele, showings will be necessary. You will have to adapt and strategize about how to keep your marketing, lead generation, follow ups, communication with clients, showings, open houses, caravans, events, and meetings in order. You will most likely be a buyer's agent the first year, working with only buyers before you get a listing. When you have a buyer looking in an area, you can attend caravans and pitch your buyer's need to all of the agents. An agent there might just have what your buyer is looking for. Caravan is an organized group of realtors who go from one home to another, viewing homes (possibly for clients) and offering feedback to the listing agent. It's quite common and something many agents take advantage of. It helps listing agents get their properties seen by local realtors and offers buyers' agents a chance to view new inventory. These are usually held weekly at specific times with the meeting held at the same location. They can easily be found online. It is recommended to attend these weekly in your area to keep track of and see new or upcoming inventory. It can come in handy if a buyer mentions what they are looking for and you just happen to know of a home coming to market that they might like.

Listen to the Lesson Learned

One of the most important lessons you will learn is to listen to what people are saying. How many times have you just wanted a salesperson to listen to what you were trying to tell them? The more you allow the prospect to talk, the more you get out of them. Remember, your job is to help them find their dream home, and the more you can learn about their needs, the better service you can provide them. You don't want to be the agent that shows 40 homes then try to make a decision on one. Think about how difficult that would be. You want to provide your clients the best customer service possible and use your time together wisely. Most people are very nervous about buying their homes and many are very scared. It is crucial to understand their fear and help them become confident in their decisions. Most importantly, don't forget to listen to what they are saying.

Follow up

Follow up is critical for your business. You want to follow up after meeting someone from open houses, listing appointments, showings, and any other interactions with clients or potential clients that you might have. You do not want to act like a salesman. You are a professional, but people want the agent they are working with to be authentic and trustworthy. It is good to let them know that you are serious in your career and will be there for them to find the perfect home or sell their home. For example, after an open house you should go to the office and pull up the list of people that signed in. Give them a call and thank them for stopping by. If you didn't get the opportunity to speak with them about their interests and what they're looking for or whether they are working with an agent, now is the perfect opportunity. Get as much information as you can from them and as they're giving you more information about the type of home they're looking for, search it in your multiple listing services and pull up a few different homes that might suit them. Bring it up to them and ask, "Have you seen the home on xxxx street? It sounds like what you're looking for." This is a great way to set up showings with them if they are not with an agent and continue a relationship. Listening comes into play once more and it is very important for you to hear what their needs are. Be sure to pay attention to details while talking to them and write down any items that are discussed so they may be addressed. On the other hand, if they say now isn't the right time or that they were just curious and started looking, stay in touch with them. Send a letter every now and then, give a call, or send an email. The agent who stays in touch will win.

Another good idea is to find out where they are in their loan process and whether they have been pre-approved. You don't want to waste your time showing houses to someone who has not been pre-approved. Most serious buyers will be pre-approved or willing to become pre-approved. This is an important step because you do not want to write an offer without knowing they can qualify for the price value. If you go out and show property, find the perfect home, put in an offer and get into escrow and then come to realize during the loan process they can't qualify for that price point, everything fails. The buyers will lose out on their deposit after removing contingencies, and you will likely lose a client and gain a bad reputation. You want to make sure your client is on track to find the right home and one of the first important steps is pre approval. This is another great way to set up an appointment with them at your office to go over the buying process. The buying process is something you should review with your broker step-by-step.

Meeting Your Client

When you meet with your potential client you can go over the process of finding a home, getting pre-approved, submitting an offer, going through escrow, and any other questions they might have. This is where knowing your contracts come in handy. You explain the process, the potential roadblocks, and a few scenarios that could occur. This is your opportunity to educate your buyer even though some may think they know it all. It's up to you to take them by the hand and walk them through the transaction. If they are still not preapproved at this point, it would be good to have one of your preferred lenders in the meeting with you. Your lender will be able to go over situations with them and explain to them the process, different financial situations, and the importance of being pre-approved. Let the client understand how you work, negotiate, keep regular communication, and can adjust strategies as needed. There may be instances where you mess up, stumble on some words, forget what to say, or other small things you might think are huge. We are human and make mistakes. Appear confident, not tentative. If they ask you a question you do not know, say, "I'm not sure, let me get the answer for you and get back to you." Make sure to write it down. Be their source for the source. Keep in mind that everything you tell them could create a liability for you. You will face many problems down the road if you try to tell them something that you are unsure of and it isn't correct. It is much easier to give the phone number or website for them to see the answer with their own eyes, and it limits your liability. Of course, when you tell them you will find out the answer, do this as quickly as possible. From this point on, you can almost be certain that you have a client who wants to trust you.

There are a few things you want to establish with your client right from the beginning of your relationship. The worst thing you would want to hear as an agent after working with someone for a few weeks is for them to say, "Thanks for all your help, I bought a house last week!" By covering some of these items, you will be more secure with them and they with you. One of the first key points to cover is loyalty. You should let them know that you will give them 100% of your effort to help them find the perfect home. However, by doing that, the only thing you ask of them is their loyalty to you. Explain to them that you are a single agent and you will represent them fairly where another agent might want to have a dual representation and not consider their best interest. Communication is key in this industry. You not only want communication with your client but also with the agent representing the seller. It would be terrible if the listing agent stole your client and was suddenly in a contract with them on the house. It is not always the case, but it is a possibility. Be sure to educate your client if they see a house they would like to view, that they should call you to make necessary arrangements. With that being said, covering the ground rules and loyalty to each other means you have to do more than what is expected. Prove to them that your word is true, and that you are loyal and dedicated to helping them find their home. As you know, without you representing them, you do not get paid.

If you want to go that extreme route and have them sign an agent representation contract, you can do so. Review the contract with your broker. Real estate is like playing a sport; you have to practice to be good, but those that put in overtime are the true professionals. Your early success should not be measured by how many transactions you close, but by how much experience, knowledge and confidence you gain as you continue advancing in your career.

Networking and Events

Another alternative and one of my favorite tactics to find new clients is various events, and specifically networking events. Stick with me, I have a little success story for you that still surprises me. I attended an event in San Diego for young entrepreneurs and other professionals who want to improve the community. I ran into a few of my friends whom I was delighted to see. As I was catching up with my friend, Keenan, a man walked up to us. As it turned out, Keenan knew him and, and he introduced me to the man. He asked me what I did for work or if I was a student, and I told him that I worked in real estate in La Jolla, and he asked me a lot of questions about the market and types of homes I worked with. At this point I was working in the luxury market. Before he left, he gave me his business card and said, "Give me a call next week, I'm thinking about selling my house." The next week, I gave him a call and we talked on the phone for a bit. He gave me his address and I told him I would generate a report of his home value and what the trend looked like for this type of home and neighborhood. It turned out to be a seven million dollar listing for me. And this all happened because I showed up to an event! Search events that interest you in your area and put them in your calendar. If they interest you, most likely it will be of interest to the other people attending, and you can find common ground and can create rapport with them.

As you prospect and begin to meet with clients, your appointments will start to become a reality. Eventually, you and your clients will pick out a few homes to see together.

There's no perfect day, time, or route you can take. When you do showings, you do want to be prepared. It is imperative that you take 30 minutes to an hour a few days before your showing to call the agent and schedule the times you will be going. Some properties may be owner occupied or others vacant. Sometimes the agent is required to meet you at the property based on seller expectations. That usually helps answer questions about the house when the listing agent is present and takes some pressure off of you. When you are setting up the showings, you usually want to set them about 30-45 minutes apart from each other, but of course that varies depending on the distance and the drive. Another key point is to align them so you aren't driving back and forth wasting time. You want to start from one end and try and work your way down the list as if you're making pit stops. Never show more than seven properties per showing appointment. Believe it or not, showing properties in one day does get tiring and you do not want to wear your client out or overwhelm them by seeing too many homes. They can get overwhelmed and confused about what exactly they want, which makes it more difficult to narrow down a home and write an offer. This is why it's important to listen and make sure you are only showing them what they want to see. If at all possible, show the best house on the list second to last. This is a small tactic if the houses they see before don't quite impress them. Once they see the house that has a majority of the features they're looking for, they will begin to realize that not all houses are going to have exactly what they want, so they need to choose the one that fits the majority of their needs. Do not try to sell them. Sometimes not speaking is more effective. The house should sell itself and speak to the buyer. Sometimes it may be difficult if the house is vacant and not staged. You may need to bring out your imagination and help them understand the possibilities.

Writing an Offer

When it comes to writing an offer, you always want to do so even if the offer is low compared to the asking price. It is your fiduciary duty to listen to your client and respect their offer. Yes, sometimes they may not get accepted or looked at, and you will receive a counter offer around 90% of the time, but you never know what the seller would agree to. Who knows, you may get them a very great deal! Also when writing the offer, you want to make sure that your clients are not offering too high or too low. You want to check comparable properties of the subject home and see what values other homes are selling for. When you are in escrow, an appraisal is ordered and an appraiser comes to the property to determine why the value was given. The appraiser makes sure the home is not being sold over market value by estimating the value of a property for tax, sales, financing, development, and insurance purposes. When you do your evaluation, look at features such as pool versus no pool, square footage, lot size, one-story or two-story, year built, and features the home includes, especially upgrades. You want to make sure you're getting the home at market value. Some buyers may not see the value and want to stay in a low range, so it is good for the buyer to understand the market for the area and see other sales.

Once you have an executed offer, you want to contact the listing agent and let them know you are sending it. The agent will present it to their seller, and you begin negotiations if it is not accepted right off the bat. Remember, all offers and counteroffers should have signatures and initials. Once your buyer and the seller agree in terms, you open escrow. Once in escrow, I recommend you at least try to handle the transaction alone for your first few times to understand the process and what is expected. There is also a transaction coordinator you can hire for a few hundred dollars or your brokerage might have an in-house transaction coordinator. From here on, you want to keep track of dates and deadlines and prepare a calendar for your escrow. One for yourself and one made for your client on deadlines for deposit, inspections, contingency removals, appraisal, loan, etc. Be sure to review this with your broker and make sure you are on track yourself.

Sellers

Now that we have mainly focused on buyers, there are also sellers who want your help. When you go to meet a seller who wants to put their home on the market, this is called a listing appointment. A day or two before meeting your potential seller, you want to put a listing presentation together. Usually your brokerage has this configured with their marketing piece, information about the brokerage, and different strategies available that will help the seller. Your job is to get the comparative market analysis, also known as CMA. You do this by searching homes in the area (usually in a half mile radius) that are similar to the subject home. Like before in our offer scenario, when you check comparables in the area, you want to focus on house size square footage, lot size, the year the house was built, upgrades, pool versus no pool, one-story or two-story, and any views if applicable. You usually go back six months to check recent sales, and you should also check active homes on the market. You want to see what price value the homes are selling at and how many days they are on the market, and be sure to call the agent to confirm any possible defects the house may have had or terms that may change the sale value such as closing costs during escrow. Always talk to a listing agent that has made a previous sale in the area. They will give you feedback on how their listing sold and pros and cons. This will be valuable not only for you when listing the home, but also for your seller to understand the current market and to get an idea of what to expect. You also want to check the active listings because the market may be starting to decrease in that area and there may not be too many buyers looking there anymore. You want to compare the price values of the active versus sold and see whether it's priced high, priced accurately, or priced very low. This will give you an idea of where the market is going for that area and where you should strategically price your home. This is something you can practice for any home and become more skilled at pricing homes by following their activity to see how accurate your analysis was. Another good tip is to go through and review your CMA and your listing agreement with your broker. You always want to take a listing agreement with you to the initial appointment, and depending on how serious your seller is, you may be able to get it signed during that meeting or at least review the terms and conditions along with your fee. If they are hesitant to sign at your appointment, here are a few good questions you can ask: Is there something I said you didn't like that's making you hesitate? What's holding you back? How serious are you? What are you looking for that I missed? Hopefully you can understand where the seller is and answer all the questions and doubts they have to make them feel confident going with you.

Walking the Home

When walking through the home, you want the seller to point out any defects they have noticed around the house, problems, or upgrades. Ask questions about the neighborhood and any other information you can get, like the amount of noise. You want to have a notepad with you when touring the house initially so you can write down what the seller is saying, as well as your own observations about the house. Be wary, you do not want to give all of your suggestions before you have a signed contract. Some sellers may use you to get that information and try and sell the home themselves. Or worse, hire a different agent. Once you have a signed contract, you always want to review what your seller can do to improve the value of the house and will appeal to buyers. This will grow for you overtime as you see more homes and understand what may be appealing for buyers. Some of the most important things are usually repainting, cleaning or installing a new carpet, hiring a professional cleaner, staging, and landscaping. If your seller decides to do anything to improve the home before putting it on the market, you want to have them set the appointments as soon as possible and create a timeline for yourself and the seller for when they will be completed. You also want to prepare photos to be taken professionally by a real estate photographer to feature on the multiple listing service and online sites. Clarify with your seller if they want any open

houses to be held or not. Before it hits the market, there is a great opportunity for you to start marking the home by word-of-mouth in your office or caravan and to any other potential buyers you have during open houses. Some sites may also allow you to post "coming soon" such as Zillow.com. You also want to feature the home on the broker's caravan for that area to have all the agents go through the home and preview it for any buyers they may have. This will create excitement for the house and you may have the possibility of selling it before it hits the market. As your fiduciary duty, you want to be clear with your seller on what is happening, what your strategies and plans are, when receiving offers what to expect when you present, and when seller wants to view offers. The seller will ask for your suggestions when reviewing offers, so make sure you prepare and view them before you send them. If you're a bit hesitant on some sections, go over them with your broker and highlight, and make sure you understand them before sending them to your seller. Ultimately your seller has the say on what they will accept, but as a professional, you should understand what a good offer for the seller would look like.

Leads and Prospects

One important tip for your career is to always keep your pipeline full. Sometimes your clients decide to take a break, or hold off until the following year, or something happens in their life that creates a hurdle. Working with one client doesn't require much time. That is why the successful agents are always busy, because they are consistently working with multiple clients. You may see some agents get a few sales in a month and then decide to take time off for the next month. Then when they return, they are at square one with no sales or contracts. If you need time, take a week and not a month.

Rentals

Some agents recommend in your first year to begin with rentals. I know some agents who mainly focus on rentals and make a good living. After a few years, the owners decide to sell and who else would they go to besides the agent that helped rent their house out and knows it best? Rentals are almost the same amount of work as a home sale. The contracts are about the same in terms and length. Although the commission might be smaller, adding a specialty in rentals can provide you with a quality source of homebuyer leads. About 35% of the U.S. population rent their homes and will be very likely to become homebuyers in the future. Depending on the neighborhood, most families will likely rent in suburban areas near a good school or a close commute to work. As their family grows, they will be looking to become more established and consider moving towards purchasing a home as stability and income increase. Like home buying, a renter is looking and testing out different areas to see what it is really like living there day to day and how it will affect them. Of course, there will also be those renters who will be getting married soon. The likelihood of them purchasing a home increases with a significant other. The rental market is filled with many different people who will buy in the future. This is a long-term business, so don't miss out on those relationships and opportunities to expand and lead to more business to create a foundation.

Referrals

Let's say you want to gain some business by referral. Great! Everyone does. But how do you do that? It is very important for all of your friends, family, classmates, sports teams, and everyone you know, to know about your new career path. Blast it on social media and include your website if you have one. Let everyone know what you do, where you focus, and how you can help them. This creates a warm lead for you if you do get any referrals from them. It advances your relationship with them and helps you move more quickly.

Another crucial step in your business is to create connections with other professionals in different fields. You want to have a relationship with another person in an industry that incorporates homes. For example, a gardener or handyman will be a good relationship like we talked about during the door knocking section. If a seller or buyer asks you for recommendations, you can refer them and be their go to real estate agent. The referrals work both ways, your clients send you referrals and your affiliate reciprocates with the same. It's a win-win solution.

Summary

What do you think so far? Doesn't sound too difficult, right? Like I mentioned in the beginning, this will be a tough job, it takes time, you will get rejected, and you might not have a paycheck for a few months. Eventually, you will gain some clientele and referrals, and your business will start to boom. Don't be afraid to mess up, it happens, we are all human and we make mistakes! After getting these basics down, there are other tactics and ways for gaining business and marketing yourself. At that point you might be able to recognize whether you're more of a direct sales or online marketing type of person. I know an agent who only sticks to online marketing and makes a killing. Whichever route you decide to go, there's always a niche you can pick and you can become a successful agent if you're consistent and hungry. There are many CRM's you can use to keep track of your clients, past clients, and reminders to follow up with future clients. I highly recommend having CRM's, and you may find one that sends email blasts for you. Start building your list with emails and phone numbers that include your sphere of influence, which are your go-to people. You will hear more about these lists through your title or broker.

Well this is it, we have come to the end of how you can start your career as a residential real estate agent. The final piece of advice I can give you is to keep track of all of your expenses. This includes all your fees for the brokerage and your license, along with meals with clients, miles driven for work, and your marketing. This will be a lifesaver when you do taxes. A great way to do this is to create an Excel document, or print and save your receipts. Last but not least, reinvest as much of your earnings in the first year back into your business and yourself in the form of education, and do something with your business every day—no matter what.

My Life

As for me, I am still learning and growing and definitely don't know it all. Real estate contains so much information and no situation is ever the same. After working as a real estate agent building my business for the first two years, I am now working at an investment company focusing on improving homes and communities around the San Diego area. I've come to realize that homes are important not only for living, but creating a lifestyle for people and families. This affects them both internally and externally. I don't want to ramble about my thoughts and feelings right now but I'd be happy to speak with you and help you anyway I can. You can always email me at Matt@MattPichardo.com. Who knows, maybe we can do a deal together! And if you've read this far, I'd be happy to be your first client as an investor and we'd be happy to have you represent us. It's time for you to crush it! There are a few tips and advice from other successful agents in the following pages you might find helpful along the way. I hope this book inspires you and gets you going in the right direction.

My warmest wishes,

Matthew Pichardo

Tips and Advice from Other Successful Agents

"For me being an agent has always been so much more than just helping clients buy and sell homes. I find that the most important thing to my clients tends to be that they know I am listening to them, hearing their needs and concerns, and understanding what their fears are about. Buying a home is such a personal decision. Whether they are first time buyers or investors, there is still that element of the client putting their trust in me, which can be daunting. Most of the time, the client already knows what they want, so it's really my job to help them achieve that final goal, whatever that might be. You must really have a love or desire to help people. If you only are interested in the paycheck, your client will sense that. It's like any industry that works with people, you must be genuine or you won't be successful or make it very long.

If this is your first year, or you're just considering getting into real estate, remember it's a people industry. Expect greatness and you will achieve it."

Candace Hart | Billionaires Row La Jolla

"You have to be READY to jump in with both feet. A lot of people get into the business because of the "flexibility" and "hours," but in order to succeed, you need to work harder than you've ever worked before (especially in years one and two). Be authentic. People are immune to spam now. I wouldn't wait to get on video. YouTube is still a wasteland of crappy realtor slideshows. Set yourself apart with QUALITY video and you will win. Interview 3+ brokerages and decide which environment is right for you. Follow up is the most important! Hire a TC for the admin, ISA for the calls, and be available to meet new people everyday and follow up with the ones that you've already met. You'll only get back what you put into it, no one is looking out for you. With three years' experience, I calendar EVERYTHING. Follow-up, content creation, and social media interactions are the #1, #2, and #3 things I focus on during the week. Always stay available all the time and be transparent. Grind your face off and you'll do well in this business. If you expect it to be easy, get out now."

Jason Cassity | City Consulting Group

"Starting out in real estate today is extremely challenging. Get out and meet as many people as you can, and involve yourself with the community as much as possible. One of the best things you can do for your business, and for your life, is to start professional coaching. This helps you with structure, balance, and running your business like a business. Make sure to schedule time off for the things you enjoy also, and know when to move on."

Brandon Weber | Weber & Weber Coastal Real Estate

"When starting out, weigh the pros and cons of joining a team. I struggled when I began because I lacked a solid mentor to give me advice and help me through even the basics of transactions. Once I joined a team, I picked up so much more, was accountable, and became more productive. Starting out, everyone will ask you how long you've been in the business. Be honest, but if you have a reputable company who backs and teaches you, leverage their name. Don't be afraid to ask "stupid" questions. Try to find the answer on your own, but if you cannot, ask. What may seem basic to an experienced agent can be frustrating for a new agent especially with acronyms (BTVABCOE?) in the MLS sheet's confidential remarks. C'mon. (Buyer to verify all before close of escrow.) Align yourself with agents that realize they too were in this place at one point and had someone helping them. If they are demeaning, ask someone willing to help. Set a schedule and stick to it. It is easy to take the day off when you make up your own schedule, but you will get out what you put in. Do what's right and do it right. There will be bad agents—ones that don't know what they're doing, rude, impossible to get in touch with, or aren't living up to their fiduciary duty. They give us a poor reputation. Don't be one of "them." You choose who you work with. But, if your clients are disrespecting you or they are draining you emotionally or financially, talk with them. If it's not mutually beneficial to work together, there are plenty more people looking to buy or sell. Find them. Take advantage of the local, regional and national organizations you're part of—online and in-person trainings, safety resources, networking. Keep a positive attitude and have fun. There will be occasional bumps, but if you enjoy what you do, you'll be able to manage them with a smile."

Arielle Hansen | Coldwell Banker Residential

"Don't expect to get paid for the first 4-7 months! Typically you will work with buyers initially and everyone's timeline differs. Remember, you are building a long-term business. Never over-promise and under-deliver. Be cautious when promising your client something that is either out of your control or may not come to fruition. Do not pretend to know something you don't know. Just tell the lead or client that you will find the answer and get back to them, they will typically understand and it is better than providing false information. Study the contract and other associated documents. If your client is the type to read every line (or a lawyer) they will expect you to know what the different paragraphs represent.

At least have a general understanding. Choose a brokerage that fits well with your personality and aligns with the type of brand you want to identify with. Interview with 3-5 different brokerages before making a decision. Every deal will be a learning experience."

Patrick Cohen | Coldwell Banker Residential

"My favorite way of prospecting is attending events and functions I am actually interested in on a personal level, not just professionally. It is so much easier to make a genuine connection with a stranger when you share the same passions! Meeting people in that capacity is a great way to establish a level of trust that could lead to an opportunity."

Danielle Hajj | Allison James Estates & Homes

"If you are going to take one day off of working, then take off Monday, because everyone complains about working Mondays."

Caroline Fores | The HomeKey Team of Berkshire Hathaway

"Tips from someone who has been there before you...FOCUS ON YOU, YOUR MARKET AND HOW TO LET THOSE PEOPLE KNOW THAT YOU EXIST (and care). Starting my career in real estate I knew only TWO things: #1. I know almost nothing about real estate except for, "location, location, location" and #2 that some people made a lot of money working in real estate. Real estate is fun, very stressful and very hands-on with almost no direction or support from anyone. Reason being? Why would I help you be an amazing agent so that you can steal potential business from ME? This is why I believe one of the most important factors in the success of a new agent is WHO you are working with. And that doesn't just mean in terms of what company you hang your license with. I mean WHO specifically you are working with, AKA a team, or a mentor. Everyone can speed up their learning curve when they are working with someone who has been somewhere or done something before they have. You can see or hear about past mistakes and TRY to avoid them yourself. For almost an entire year I worked at Berkshire Hathaway, one of the most respected company names on the planet and I made only $2,500 dollars. Not $25,000.00, which still would have been pretty poor performance. I mean Two thousand and five hundred dollars over an 11-month period. By month 12 I had been recruited (luckily) to another brokerage working with a broker who truly knew what it meant to hustle, make money, and make deals happen. In the next 8 months I had made over $50,000 and was exposed to a whole new level of business. This brings me to my second piece of advice, HUSTLE. And I do not mean hustle in terms of pulling fast ones on people and getting deals done at the expense of others (or even worse of your reputation). Money will come and go, as will business, but one thing that will stick around is a bad reputation. If people think you are lazy, stupid, or generally unreliable and untrustworthy, you will not be referred (which is a massive and reliable part of this business). Real estate, no matter how big of a city you are in, is a small community where 80% of the deals get done by 20% of the hustlers. Put yourself in your client's' shoes and walk a mile. Would you want an agent that waits for opportunities and then simply shows you what's available online? Or would you want an agent who knows almost every owner or business in the marketplace and has a real focus on the bigger picture? Needless to say we'd all choose the latter."

Kyle Erthner | UrbanCalifornia

"Consistency is key and patience is a virtue—whatever you do, commit to it and be persistent until it starts to pay off. Therefore, before you commit to doing something, make sure it's something you're going to be able to stick to and give it a fair chance. Usually efforts in this business take six months to a year or even more before work starts to pay off. Treat it like a job—it's so easy to slack off in this job because you don't have to clock in or out. Have a set schedule and do your best to stick to it. Know your style. Don't try to do everything at first. Pick one form of prospecting, two at most, and get really good at it/them. Whether it's cold calling, open houses, door knocking, etc., I would say just try to master one thing. Otherwise, you will waste time and money, and you will feel like you're spread too thin and you won't benefit as much as you would if you just did one thing well and consistently! Beware of mailers: they get expensive and they take time to create and more time to show you a return. If you do them, double up in that farm with open houses and door knocking in the exact same place you're mailing. Otherwise, you will probably be throwing money away. Face-to-face or active prospecting (i.e.: cold calling) are always better in my opinion. KNOW THE CONTRACT and shadow an agent on a deal from start to finish so you know the process. Just because you have your license, it doesn't mean you know how to open and close a deal."

Natalie Harris | Coldwell Banker La Jolla

"I would say for me, consistency was (still is) the most important factor for any real estate agent new or seasoned. It takes a while to accomplish goals and build a good, growing business. Whether it's open houses, door knocking, or direct mail campaigns, it's important to consistently do them. It may take a month, two months, six months or a year to really get the results you're looking for, but don't give up if you see no or little results early. Most realtors do and that's why they fail. Some agents bounce around from idea to idea and it results in nothing because they want or need that instant gratification. Take time and pride in your craft and with hard work all will be good! When I first started as an agent all the other realtors intimidated me. I thoughteveryone knew more than me (they didn't) and looked at me like another newbie (some do, most don't). I never really went to the networking events or tried to meet other realtors/agents and that was a big mistake on my part. It took me a little over a year to realize that. The people you know and the people who know you can and will only enhance your business. I landed a deal once because the agent knew me, saw I worked hard and accepted our offer over another (same price, same terms). I would have stopped my "too cool for school" attitude earlier. One more would be to try different things in the beginning and see what you like or what you're best at. When you do something you love in a manner you enjoy, people notice that and will be drawn to you. Life is short and work should be fun, although tough and stressful sometimes, but ultimately enjoyable. I wake up every day loving what I do and my growing business shows that."

David Spiewak | Coldwell Banker La Jolla

"Important Lesson: Don't give up on deals, people, or houses. Always look for solutions to the problems, instead of just giving up escrows, when things go south. As for marketing, my most important advice I could ever give is to start organizing, marketing, and systematizing your sphere of influence as soon as you get your license. Create a system, and follow it consistently. It will be your golden goose. I would join a successful team and learn from the big wigs. I have reinvented the wheel with my business and it took me so much time, effort, and emotional investment to figure things out on my own. I would have been successful much sooner and learned a lot faster if I had just joined the team instead. Your first year in the business you should be with a very well known company that has a strong training and mentorship program. MINDSET is the most important thing you should always control. Always keep learning, flexibility and persistence. You can expect to fail a lot. Your deals fall through, buyers won't buy and sellers won't sell, and escrows will cancel. It's ok and it is part of the business. Remember this. After seven years in the business, I like to plan my week on Sunday night. You should set the number of people you will have to contact, appointments you will have, and other prospecting activities. Prospecting is KING, the rest is secondary. My week consists of prospecting, current client care, education, and social events. You will find clients by prospecting. There are a hundred or more ways to get clients in real estate, whether it's cold calling, door knocking, mailing, events, networking, open houses, etc. Pick 2-3 that you like and stick to it religiously for a year. Then track your results, then adjust and reinvent, if needed, or repeat, if it was successful. Be responsive when you have clients. Get back to them ASAP. Be proactive, but never put your commission above their ultimate good. It's an amazing business, where you can make a 6-figure income and be your own boss without much education or a lot of financial investment. It's a brilliant business, but like everything else in life, your success directly correlates with the amount of work and effort you put into it. Don't give up. Create a structure around you, whether it's coaching, a mentor, a paid system, etc. and follow it consistently. You can get what you want out of it."

Khrystyna Chorna | Pacific Sotheby's International Realty

"Relationships are the cornerstone of any business, particularly the business of real estate. For both beginners and veteran agents alike, relationships are the foundation on which success is built—and maintained. I've learned that the two most important relationships are the relationship you have with your mentor, and the relationship you have with your peers. I've learned how incredibly beneficial it is to find a mentor who will guide you through your first few transactions and who will nurture your learning process. During the beginning of your career, acting as an apprentice to an experienced agent will encourage personal and business growth. In addition to building a relationship with a mentor, it's also crucial to establish a rapport with your peers, community and, ultimately, develop a strong sphere of influence. Get connected. Get involved. Get to know your community. Most importantly, have fun!"

Elyse Dittrich | Nancarrow Realty Group, Inc.

Thank You for Purchasing My Book!

I really appreciate all of your feedback, and I love hearing what you have to say.

Please leave me a helpful review on Amazon letting me know what you thought of the book.

*Thanks so much and **GO GET EM!!***

Made in the USA
Middletown, DE
27 April 2020